Tai Chi Qigong Shibashi

Set 1 & 2

Sifu Wing Cheung

ISBN: 978-1-0691297-3-4

Table of Contents

About the Author

Sifu (Master) Wing Cheung is the founder of the Tai Chi, Qigong, and Feng Shui Institute. He began learning various martial arts, including Tai Chi—an internal martial art that utilizes qi (energy)—at the age of six under the guidance of his father. who was both a Kung Fu and Tai Chi master and the champion of the 1969 Canton Province Kickboxing Championship. Following in his father's footsteps, Sifu Wing Cheung also became a champion, winning the Tai Chi Division of the 2005 National Kung Fu and Wushu Championship.

In 1994, a serious traffic accident marked a turning point in Sifu Cheung's life. Seeking recovery, he turned to Master Wu Jian Hua, a renowned Qi healer. Under Master Wu's mentorship, he immersed himself in acupressure, traditional Chinese medicine, and various styles of Qigong (exercise or practice for cultivating qi). This transformative experience led him to leave his promising career in the financial industry to pursue the ancient healing arts and share their benefits with the public.

Sifu Cheung's first international teaching tour in 2006

In 2003, another life-changing event inspired Sifu Cheung to explore the deeper spiritual dimensions of energy practices. Over the next decade, he traveled worldwide to study various energy and spiritual traditions, including Tibetan Buddhism, Shaolin Neigong, Daoist Inner Alchemy, Kriya Yoga, and Vipassana meditation.

His spiritual quest culminated in 2013 when he was initiated by Master Gordon Pang into a profound spiritual lineage, as well as the Dan Ding and Tai Chi Gates—two of the Five Secret Gates of Daoism (You can learn more about the 5

Secret Gates of Daoism from this video: https://youtu.be/r3x4nA14k70 , start watching from the 21 minutes mark.) From September 2018 to March 2024, Sifu Cheung paused his global teaching tours to focus on personal retreats, further deepening his spiritual and Qi practices.

Sifu Cheung's first workshop after his 5½ year retreat in 2024

Sifu Wing Cheung has dedicated his life to sharing the wonders of Qi with people worldwide. Through his workshops, he has trained and certified thousands of Tai Chi Qigong instructors. His teaching emphasizes not only the physical aspects of these arts but also the development of subtle internal skills. To support his students, he has created and refined a variety of Qigong and healing programs designed to accelerate learning and empower individuals in their self-healing journeys.

In addition to teaching Tai Chi, Qigong, and traditional Daoist Neigong, Sifu Cheung is an accomplished Feng Shui consultant. His online programs and in-person workshops offer structured pathways for students at all levels, and he occasionally hosts specialized Tai Chi and Qigong camps for advanced practitioners.

Introduction to Tai Chi Qigong Shibashi

Tai Chi Qigong Shibashi was born in the years following China's Cultural Revolution (1968–1976), a turbulent era that saw practices like Qigong, Tai Chi, and Traditional Chinese Medicine (TCM) banned. This suppression, however, couldn't extinguish the ancient wisdom rooted in the fabric of these ancient arts. When the restrictions ended, China entered what is now known as the "Qigong Fever" period. During this time, hundreds of Qigong styles emerged or were revitalized in the span of about a decade.

While many of these styles remained obscure or gradually faded into obscurity, Tai Chi Qigong Shibashi became a rare and enduring exception. Its popularity soared, thanks to its simplicity, accessibility, and profound health benefits. Tai Chi Qigong Shibashi consists of just 18 movements—hence the name *Shibashi*, which translates to "18 movements." Despite being simpler than the 24-form Simplified Tai Chi created in 1956, this practice has proven to deliver faster and more noticeable health benefits for many practitioners.

Much like the collaborative effort that created the 24-form Simplified Tai Chi, Tai Chi Qigong Shibashi Set 1 and Set 2 were developed in 1980 by a team of masters with extensive backgrounds in Qigong, Tai Chi, and Wushu. This group was led by Lin Housheng, Zhu Longmei, Lin Ping, Gu Qun, Xue Laidi, and He Weiqi. Their combined expertise resulted in a form that beautifully integrates the principles of Tai Chi with the energetic flow of Qigong.

The Global Rise of Tai Chi Qigong Shibashi

Soon after its creation, Tai Chi Qigong Shibashi captured the hearts of millions. Across China and Southeast Asia, it became a common sight to see hundreds, even thousands, of people practicing this Qigong daily in stadiums and parks. Its simplicity and effectiveness made it a favorite choice for people of all ages and backgrounds. In fact, the practice became so widespread that both Malaysia and Indonesia officially recognized it as a national exercise.

While its prominence in Asia has shifted over time, Tai Chi Qigong Shibashi has found a new audience in the West. In countries like the United Kingdom, this Qigong form has been introduced into schools, hospitals, and even prisons, thanks to its accessibility and proven health benefits. Its gentle yet effective movements make it a preferred option for enhancing physical and mental well-being in various institutional settings.

Hundreds practicing Tai Chi Qigong Shibashi in a stadium in Malaysia

A Personal Journey with Tai Chi Qigong Shibashi

Tai Chi Qigong Shibashi is the very first Qigong I learned, taught by Master Wu Jian Hua, a renowned Qigong healer. Master Wu was a colleague of Master Lin Housheng, the lead creator of Tai Chi Qigong Shibashi, at the Shanghai Qigong Research Institute. Together, they conducted numerous Qi-related experiments, exploring the boundaries of what Qigong could achieve in healing and human potential.

By the time I began teaching Qigong publicly in 2000, I had already mastered over ten different styles of Qigong. While Tai Chi Qigong Shibashi was not the most powerful qigong I have taught, it has remained a favorite among my students.

Why Tai Chi Qigong Shibashi is So Popular

The enduring popularity of Tai Chi Qigong Shibashi can be attributed to several key factors:

A. Ease of Learning

Tai Chi Qigong Shibashi Set 1 is remarkably easy to learn, especially for beginners. Most of its movements are performed in a stationary position, making it accessible even to individuals with mild mobility issues. For example, in a one-hour class, I can typically teach three movements. This approachable pace makes it ideal for newcomers, enabling steady progress without feeling overwhelmed. In contrast, some traditional Tai Chi movements, such as "Repulsing Monkey," often require two one-hour classes to master due to the complexity of dynamic stepping.

For those unable to practice standing, I have also created a seated version of the Shibashi movements, ensuring that even individuals with significant physical limitations can benefit from this practice. The sequence of movements is also easier to remember compared to the Tai Chi Simplified 24 Form, further lowering the barrier to entry.

Additionally, you do not need a lot of space to practice Tai Chi Qigong Shibashi—just 1 square meter is enough. This makes it an ideal practice for individuals living in tiny apartments or small spaces.

Seated Version of Shibashi Set 1

B. Safety and Gentleness

Tai Chi Qigong Shibashi is one of the safest and most gentle forms of aerobic exercise. Over the years, I have taught this form to tens of thousands of people, none have ever experienced injuries from practicing this gentle Qigong. This safety is unparalleled, even when compared to activities as simple as fast walking, which carries the risk of tripping and falling.

Despite its gentle nature, Tai Chi Qigong Shibashi qualifies as a mild-impact aerobic exercise. Many are surprised they sweat after performing these seemingly soft movements. The movements, which often involve raising and lowering the body, are akin to performing slow, semi-squats for over ten minutes. This strengthens the legs, improves cardiovascular health, and stimulates the secretion of positive hormones like endorphins, which promote relaxation and a sense of well-being.

C. The Qi Connection

Among all the Qigong styles I've encountered, Tai Chi Qigong Shibashi Set 1 is the easiest for practitioners to feel the Qi. This is a transformative moment for many students, as feeling Qi for the first time often ignites a deep passion for continued practice. It was this very sensation that first hooked me into Qigong decades ago, and it remains a powerful motivator for new practitioners.

Shibashi is also an excellent supplementary exercise to enhance practices like Reiki, meditation, and Tai Chi. I have a few students who are Reiki Masters, and they report feeling their energy much stronger after Shibashi practice. The same is true for meditation: when Qi flows smoothly in the body, one can easily sit still for over an hour, making it easier to enter Samadhi.

As for Tai Chi, I would estimate that over 90% of practitioners cannot feel the Qi. However, once they experience the sensation of Qi through Shibashi, it elevates their Tai Chi practice to a whole new level. For this reason, more and more Tai Chi schools are adopting Shibashi as a warm-up exercise.

D. Health Benefits and Healing Power

The health benefits of Tai Chi Qigong Shibashi are often noticeable within a few months, and in some cases, even after just one class. This Qigong is particularly effective for individuals suffering from chronic and degenerative diseases.

According to Traditional Chinese Medicine, there are two main causes of illness:

1. **Insufficient Qi**

   Qi, often referred to as the body's life force or energy, is essential for maintaining vitality, health, and balance. As we age, our Qi levels gradually diminish. This decline is a natural process, much like the wear and tear on our physical body.

   External factors like poor diet, injuries, chronic stress, and environmental pollution can further deplete our Qi reserves, accelerating the aging process and increasing vulnerability to illness. When Qi levels become too low, the body struggles to sustain optimal function, leading to a range of physical, mental, and emotional imbalances.

   When practicing Tai Chi Qigong Shibashi it is important to enter the "Qigong mind state"—a relaxed and meditative mindset— which allows Qi to flow naturally into the body, revitalizing energy stores. Thus, regular practice helps counteract the depletion of Qi, effectively slowing down the aging process and improving overall well-being.

2. **Blocked Meridians**

The second cause of illness, according to Traditional Chinese Medicine, is blocked meridians. Meridians are the pathways through which Qi flows which connects to vital organs, much like rivers carrying water to nourish the land. When the body is tense, these meridians constrict, impeding the natural flow of Qi. Over time, this blockage prevents Qi to nourish our organs which lead to many problems.

The key to unblocking these pathways lies in relaxation and mindful movement. In Tai Chi Qigong Shibashi, each movement is performed in a gentle, fluid, and relaxed manner, encouraging the meridians to open naturally. The combination of mental focus and physical relaxation allows Qi to flow freely along these pathways. As the Qi flows back and forth during practice, it gradually dissolves blockages, restoring harmony and vitality to the body.

Like clearing a clogged pipe, this process requires patience and consistent effort. Over time, the accumulated tension and blockages are gradually released, restoring the body's natural balance. This is why practitioners often report feeling lighter, more energized, and mentally clearer after practicing Tai Chi Qigong Shibashi regularly.

Understanding Qi

For those new to Qigong, the concept of Qi may seem abstract or mysterious. Simply put, Qi is often described as the life force or energy that sustains all living things. It flows through us and connects us to the universe. While ancient wisdom has long recognized its existence, modern science is just beginning to explore its properties.

While scientific experiments have detected some measurable aspects of Qi, such as infrared radiation, magnetic fields, and infrasonic waves, these findings have yet to fully grasp its full picture. Qi represents a holistic phenomenon that bridges the physical and spiritual realms. That's why scientists have developed devices to mimic certain frequencies and intensities of Qi emitted by Qigong healers, the results, though somewhat effective, are still far from replicating the true effects of an accomplished Qi healer because one key component is missing, the intention of the healer.

The Purpose of This Book

My goal in writing this book is not to overwhelm you with theories or scientific studies but to guide you in the practical application of Tai Chi Qigong Shibashi. The true benefits of Qigong come from practice, not from reading or intellectualizing. As you follow the instructions in this book, you will gradually experience the health benefits for yourself.

If you are interested in exploring the theoretical aspects of Qigong and Tai Chi further, I encourage you to sign up for our free newsletter at **taichi18.com**. This resource is an excellent gateway to deeper understanding and offers additional exercises to complement your practice. For a more structured exploration of the principles behind Qigong and Tai Chi, consider our Qigong Mode and Tai Chi Postures Requirements courses. These courses provide valuable insights into the foundations of energy work and movement.

Enhancing the Practice

Drawing from my background in Tai Chi and meditation, I have infused the original Shibashi practice with more Tai Chi elements and mindfulness. This adaptation enhances the meditative quality of the movements, making it feel like a flowing, moving meditation which further amplifies its healing potential. Many of my students have remarked that this approach transforms the practice, allowing them to reach deeper levels of relaxation and inner peace.

Final Thoughts

Tai Chi Qigong Shibashi is more than just an exercise—it is a journey of self-discovery and healing. By practicing regularly, you are not only nurturing your body but also cultivating a deeper connection to the life force that sustains you. Whether you are seeking relief from illness, a way to manage stress, or simply a path to greater vitality, this Qigong practice has the potential to transform your life.

Remember, the key to success lies in consistency. Even just 15–20 minutes of daily practice can yield significant results over time. Let Tai Chi Qigong Shibashi become a part of your daily routine, and you will soon discover the profound joy and tranquility it brings.

I invite you to embark on this journey with an open mind and heart. Follow the instructions in this book, allow yourself to feel the Qi, and watch as your body, mind, and spirit align in harmony.

Sifu Wing Cheung

How to Practice

Where to practice: This type of qigong can be practiced indoors or outdoors. A quiet and peaceful environment with good air circulation should be chosen. Avoid practicing outside during severe weather such as thunderstorms or strong winds, or on days with high smog alerts.

Breathing: The type of breathing we will be doing throughout this qigong exercise is called abdominal breathing. Abdominal breathing is breathing using your diaphragm. You inhale through your nose and exhale through your mouth (it is ok to exhale through the nose too if this is your habit). It is called abdominal breathing because the movement of your diaphragm will expand your lower abdomen during the inhale and contract your lower abdomen during the exhale. Breathe deeply using the full extent of your lung capacity.

How to start: This qigong is very effective and easy to learn. However, you should not expect to remember all 18 movements at one time. You should begin by practicing the first 3 movements. When these 3 movements have been mastered, proceed to practicing the next 3 movements in addition to the first 3 that you have just mastered.

There is poster available https://taichi18.com/shop/page/2/ to help you remember the 18 movements and their sequence. When practiced regularly, most people will be able to master all 18 movements within a week. You should start to see some results when you practice on a daily basis for three months.

Here is the link to the Tai Chi Qigong Shibashi Set 1 Video: https://youtu.be/JHQmY2sLhbI

Opening Position (Wuji Stance)

- stand with feet shoulder width apart
- relax the whole body
- arms hang down at sides
- palms face thighs
- knees bend slightly
- clear the mind
- remain in this posture for a few minutes

Common Mistakes:

1. Squeeze the armpits

Make sure there is some space in your armpits. If you squeeze your armpits, the energy will have a difficult time flowing between your arms and body.

Make sure your body is upright, straight and centered.

As you go through this qigong exercise all movements are gentle and flow seamlessly from one to the next in coordination with your breathing.

1. Commencing Form

A. Raise arms out front to shoulder level:

- breathing in
- palms face back
- fingers point down and are slightly curved
- raise body by straightening legs
- bring arms up to shoulder height and width
- palms face down

B. Return arms down to sides:

- breathing out
- turn palms to face forwards
- fingers point up and are slightly curved
- bend elbows
- sink body down with knees bent
- lower arms back down
- palms at thigh level facing back

Repeat A-B 6 times

The purpose of this movement is to pump the qi out from the lower dan tian (just below navel), so that it can travel throughout the whole body. Tai chi Chuan and many other martial arts begin with this movement in order to activate the energy from the lower dan tian.

Common Mistakes:

1. Feet pointing outwards

Make sure your feet are parallel and pointing forwards.

2. Pelvis not relaxed

Make sure your spine is straight, and your knees do not go beyond the toes.

3. Arms not parallel

Make sure your arms are parallel to each other.

4. Elbows and wrists are not relaxed when pressing down

Elbows and wrists bend slightly as the arms are
moving up or down.

5. Bending the neck

Make sure your spine is straight, and your head is aligned with your spine.

6. Moving the arms only

Many students just move their arms and forget about moving the whole body. Make sure the whole body moves up and down in coordination with the arms.

Visualization for your arms:

When your arms are coming up, make sure they are very relaxed. They should feel light as if they are floating in the air. You can visualize that there are wires attached to your wrists. When your arms go up, the wires are lifting your arms up, so that they rise effortlessly.

When you press down, visualize you are pressing them onto the water; so that you feel some resistance. Then, totally relax your arms, and let them sink slowly by themselves.

2. Broadening One's Chest

A. Raise arms out front to shoulder level:

- breathing in
- palms face back
- fingers point down and are slightly curved
- raise body
- arms come up to shoulder height and width
- palms face down

B. Open arms out to sides:

- turn palms to face each other
- open arms out to the sides
- arms fully extended out to the sides

C. Close arms in front:

- breathing out
- bring hands together (palms facing) until shoulder width apart

D. Return arms down to sides:

- turn palms to face the front
- fingers up and slightly curved
- bend elbows
- sink body down with knees bent
- lower arms back down
- palms at thigh level facing back

Repeat A-D 6 times

Common Mistakes:

1. Doing steps A and B simultaneously

Make sure your arms come up first and then open out.

2. Doing steps C and D simultaneously

Make sure to close your arms in front first and then press down.

3. Arms open too wide

Your hands should not go beyond the sides of your body.

Visualization:

For this movement, you can visualize you are standing on top of a mountain and breathing in the fresh air.

3. Dancing with Rainbows

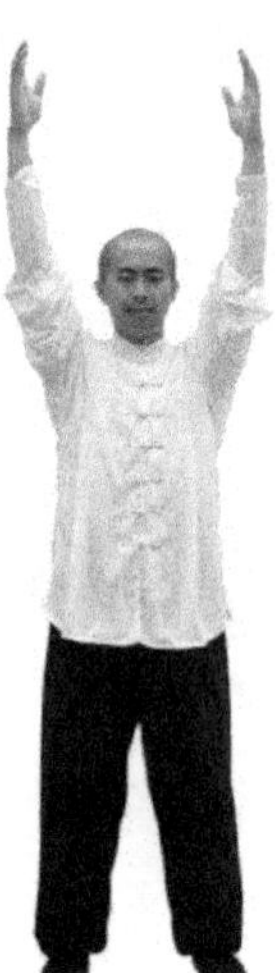

Breathing in, raise body and arms.
Raise arms all the way up and then turn palms to face each other.

A. Turn to the left:

- breathing in
- transfer body weight to right leg by bending right leg slightly
- extend left arm out to left side at shoulder height, palm up
- turn head to look left
- eyes focus on extended left palm
- curve right arm over head so palm faces down above center of head

B. Turn to the right:

- breathing out
- transfer body weight to left leg by bending left leg slightly
- extend right arm out to right side at shoulder height, palm up
- turn head to look right
- eyes focus on extended right palm
- curve left arm over head so left palm faces down above center of head

Repeat A-B 6 times

1. Stopping when reaching the end of the movement

Do not stop between steps A and B. Make sure transitions are smooth and the movements are continuous.

2. Arms not moving together

Make sure both arms are moving at the same time.

3. Shifting weight to the wrong side

Make sure your weight is on the opposite side of your arm outstretched arm.

4. Shuffling the feet

The feet should not move.

5. Twisting and turning the upper body

Your body should remain straight and facing the front, just naturally move sideways when you shift your weight.

6. Outstretched arm dropping too low

Make sure your outstretched arm is at your shoulder height.

7. Palm not facing center of head

8. Shoulders are raised

Make sure your shoulders are relaxed. If you raise your shoulders during this movement, the qi will be blocked, and your shoulders will get tired just after a few moves.

To check if your shoulder is raised or not:

Put your fingers on top of your collar bone and
then raise your arm. If your shoulder remains
relaxed, this bone will not tilt up.

If you raise your shoulder, this bone will tilt up.

Visualization:

Your *lao gong* is the acupoint on the center of your palm and the *bai hui* is the
acupoint on top of your head.

As you move your hand upwards, visualize you are scooping up all the good qi
and positive energy. When your right hand reaches the top of your head, the *lao
gong* should face the *bai hui* so that the positive energy travels downward to fill
your whole body.

Visualize the same on the other side. Scoop up the qi. When your *lao gong* faces
your *bai hui*, it fills your whole body with the good qi.

4. Circling Arms

Shift weight back to center. Lower arms in front of body, palms face each other.

A. Cross hands in front:

- breathing in
- turn palms to face up
- cross hands at wrists with right hand over left

B. Raise arms:

- raise body slightly
- palms face body
- raise the arms until palms reach face level

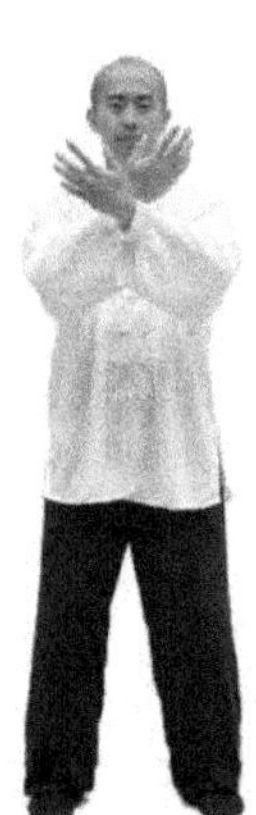

C. Turn palms out:

- turn palms to face away from body
- raise arms above head

D. Lower arms:

- breathing out
- hands separate and circle out to sides
- palms face out
- extended arms continue to circle downwards
- palms face down

Repeat A-D 6 times

Common Mistakes:

1. Palms not facing body

When you raise your arms, your palms face your body.

2. Bending or arching the neck

Your eyes can look up or down following your hands, but do not bend or arch your neck. Make sure your spine is straight so that the energy will have an easier time flowing in your body.

3. Palms cross at wrong position

They should cross at the 'inner gate'.

Inner Gate:

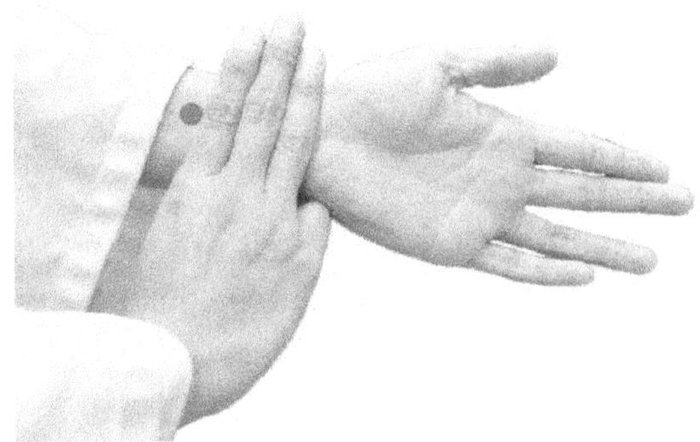

The *inner gate* is located at the middle of your arm, 3 fingers below the wrist line.

This acupoint is very important because the number 1 killer of the world is heart disease. If you stimulate this point often enough, it can prevent heart disease and regulate blood pressure.

To stimulate this point, simply use your thumb to press it down for 2 seconds, release for 2 seconds. Repeat the above step for about 5 minutes, then do the same thing for the other hand. You may do this 2-4 times a day. When you press it correctly, you should feel some sensation along your palm to your middle finger.

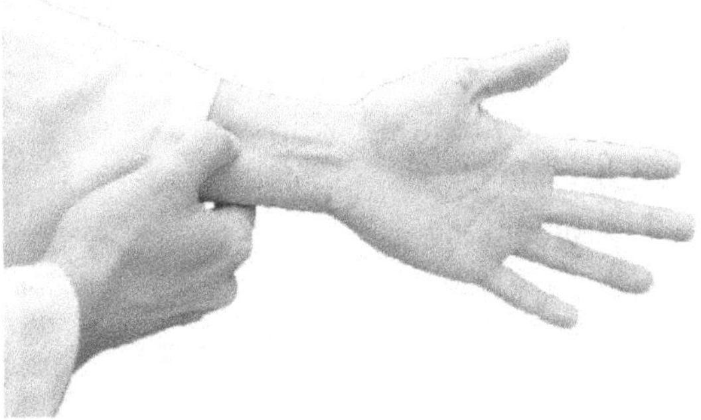

You can do this at any time or place; for example, while travelling on a bus or plane, watching TV, or whenever you have spare time.

5. Twisting Waist & Swing Arms

Turn palms to face up and raise arms out front to
shoulder level.

Remain in horse riding stance throughout the
entire movement.

A. Turn to right:

- breathing in
- bend right elbow with forearm parallel to
  the ground
- pull right arm back
- turn body from waist toward the right
- slowly spiral left palm so that it faces up
  when the arm is fully extended (skip this
  step during the first repetition)

B. Lower forearm:

- Lower right forearm when body completely
  turned to the right

C. Circle right hand back and up to ear:

- draw right arm up in an arc behind body
- continue to extend the right arm back then up, palm up
- palm tip at ear height
- turn right palm to face the front

D. Push right hand:

- breathing out
- turn body from waist back to center
- push right hand forward
- simultaneously draw left arm towards body
- palms cross in front of chest (right over left), about 2 fists away from the body

E. Turn to left:

- breathing in
- bend left elbow with forearm parallel to the ground
- pull left arm back
- turn body from waist toward the left
- slowly spiral right palm to the front so that it faces up when the arm is fully extended

F. Lower forearm:

- Lower left forearm when body completely turned to the left

G. Circle left hand back and up to ear

- draw left arm up in an arc behind body
- continue to extend the left arm back then up, palm up
- palm tip at ear height
- turn left palm to face the front

H. Push left hand to front:

- breathing out
- turn body from waist back to center
- push left hand forward
- simultaneously draw right arm towards body
- palms cross in front of chest (left over right), about 2 fists away from the body

Repeat A-H 3 times

Common Mistakes:

1. Skipping one of the steps, in particular steps B and F

Be sure to complete all steps.

2. Moving up and down

You should remain in the horse-riding stance throughout the entire movement.

3. Moving from the lower body

You should turn from your waist instead of turning from your lower body. If you turn from your waist, the knees are not moving much. This stimulates your belt meridian. The belt meridian is like a belt around your waist. All the other meridians are more or less vertical going up and down. This belt meridian circles around all the other meridians. When this belt meridian is stimulated, it means all the other meridians get stimulated as well.

4. Not spiraling the hand when pushing out

Make sure the hand pushing out starts spiraling
after it crosses the other hand.

5. Squeeze the armpits

Make sure there is some space in your armpits.

6. Shoulder is raised when doing steps C and G

Visualization:

You may visualize that there is an energy
ball on your palm. When your palms meet
at the center of your body, you drop the
ball onto the other hand. Your breathing
changes when the ball changes hands, and
your eyes follow the ball.

6. Rowing a Boat

Turn palms to face downwards and lower both arms to the sides.

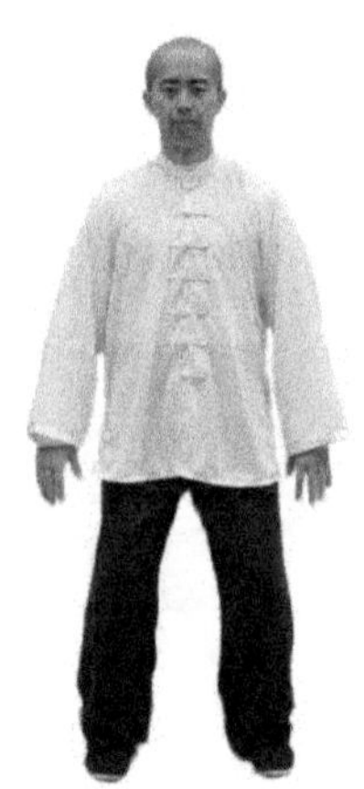

A. Raise arms over head:

- breathing in
- raise body
- circle arms back then up (palms face back then up as arms go up)
- hands extend above head, palms facing front

B. Lower arms in front:

- breathing out
- sink body down with knees slightly bent
- circle arms down to slightly past the thighs
- palms face down then back

Repeat A-B 6 times

Common Mistakes:

1. Arms not straight when pressing down

Do not bend your elbows when pressing down, but make sure your elbows are not locked. This means your arms look relatively straight but are not 100% straight; your elbows are still relaxed. Remember, in all the other movements, your knees are never 100% straight either. When you go up, your knees are still bent a little bit; maybe 99% straight but never 100%.

2. Turning the arms too early

Make sure your arms go past your body before you lift and turn your arms.

7. Holding a Ball

Raise body.

A. Turn to the left:

- breathing in
- turn body from waist toward the left
- extend right arm up across body to the left until shoulder height, palm up
- left hand is slightly behind left thigh, facing back
- raise both heels; right heel rises higher (weight is mostly on the left foot)

B. Lower heels:

- breathing out
- lower heels to the ground
- turn right palm downwards
- slightly bend knees
- turn body from waist back to center
- lower right arm down to thigh

C. Turn to the right:

- breathing in
- turn body from waist toward the right
- extend left arm up across body to the right until shoulder height, palm up
- right hand is slightly behind right thigh, facing back
- raise both heels, left heel rises higher (weight is mostly on the right foot)

D. Lower heels:

- breathing out
- lower heels to the ground
- turn left palm downwards
- slightly bend knees
- turn body from waist back to center
- lower left arm down to thigh

Repeat A-D 3 times

Common Mistakes:

1. Leaning forward

Make sure your body is upright and straight.

2. Pause between steps A & B or C & D

Make sure the movements are continuous.

3. Not turning the body

You are not just lifting your arms sideways.
Make sure you are turning your body from
the waist.

4. Not turning enough

You should turn sideways 90 degrees, not 45
degrees.

8. Carrying the Moon

A. Turn to the left:

- breathing in
- raise body
- turn body from waist towards the left
- extend left arm 45 degrees up and toward the back
- head looks at left hand
- right palm faces left armpit

B. Return to center:

- breathing out
- turn body from waist back to center
- sink body down with knees slightly bent
- lower arms down and to the front in line with thighs
- palms facing each other hip width apart

C. Turn to the right:

- breathing in
- raise body
- turn body from waist towards the right
- extend right arm 45 degrees up and toward the back
- head looks at right hand
- left palm faces right armpit

D. Return to center:

- breathing out
- turn body from waist back to center
- sink body down with knees slightly bent
- lower arms down and to the front in line with thighs (for the final repetition skip this part
- palms facing each other hip width apart (for the final repetition skip this part)

Repeat A-D 3 times

Common Mistakes:

1. Bending body forward

When your arms come down, do not bend your body forward. Make sure your body is upright.

2. Palm not facing armpit

3. Arms not turning high or far enough

How far you want to turn is up to you, but make sure you are not just bringing your arms 90 degrees out to the side. They should be towards the back as far as is comfortable. Ideally, you should turn 180 degrees to the back, with arms 45 degrees up.

Visualization:

You may visualize that you are carrying a big energy ball; then sending it into the sky, to the very far of the universe.

9. Twisting Waist & Pushing Hands

Bring left hand, palm up, to the left side of waist; right hand in front of right shoulder.

A. Push to left:

- breathing out
- turn right palm to face forwards
- turn body from waist towards the left
- push right hand to left at 45 degrees and up to chest level
- shift weight to left leg about 70%

B. Return to center:

- breathing in
- turn body from waist back to center
- slowly turn right palm up
- draw right hand back to right side of waist

C. Push to right:

- breathing out
- turn left palm faces to face forwards
- turn body from waist toward right
- push left hand to right at 45 degrees and up to chest level
- shift weight to right leg about 70%

D. Return to center:

- breathing in
- turn body from waist back to center
- slowly turn left palm up (for the final repetition skip this part)
- draw left hand back to left side of waist (for the final repetition skip this part)

Repeat A-D 3 times

Common Mistakes:

1. Weight on wrong side

When you push out, your stance becomes a bow stance. Weight distribution is about 70-30. Make sure your weight is on the same side of where you are pushing.

2. Pushing sideways

You are pushing 45 degrees, not 90 degrees.

3. Over-extending

Make sure your body is upright, not leaning.

4. Palms too high

Your palms should be resting at your waist
level, not your chest level.

Visualization:

As you push, you can visualize you are pushing to the very far corner of the room.
This is a very good way to train your intention.

10. Playing with Clouds

Raise left hand to throat level, palm faces body and is about 3 fists away from the body.

Turn right palm to faces body at waist level and is about 2 fists away from the body.

Remain in horse riding stance throughout the entire movement.

A. Turn to the left:

* breathing in
* turn body from waist toward the left
* allow arms to follow turn

B. Switch positions of the arms:

* raise right hand to throat level, palm faces body and is about 3 fists away from the body
* drop left hand to waist level, palm faces body and is about 2 fists away from the body

C. Turn to the right:

* breathing out
* turn body from waist toward the right
* allow arms to turn with waist

D. Switch positions of the arms:

- raise left hand to throat level, palm faces body and is about 3 fists away from the body
- drop right hand to waist level, palm faces body and is about 2 fists away from the body

Repeat A-D 6 times (skip step D at final repetition)

Common Mistakes:

1. Shoulders and elbows not relaxed

2. Squeeze the armpits

Make sure there is some space in your armpits.

3. Palms not facing the body

In traditional tai chi cloud hands, the palms are facing out; but this is qigong, the palms should be facing your body.

4. Turning from lower body

You are turning from your waist. You should remain in the horse riding stance throughout the entire movement, so minimize the knee movements.

11. Scooping from the Sea

Place left foot a half step forward.

A. Bend forward:

- transfer weight to the left foot
- bend at the waist bringing both arms down towards the left foot
- cross hands, right over left, over the left foot
- palms are facing up
- top of the head aligns with the left foot

B. Scoop up:

- breathing in
- transfer weight to right leg
- gradually straighten body upright
- bring crossed palms up above head

C. Separate hands:

- breathing out (skip this part for the final repetition)
- separate and circle extended arms out to the sides then down
- palms face down

Repeat A-C 6 times

Common Mistake:

Not bending the forward leg when moving down

When you move forward, make sure your weight is on the left leg, so the left keen is bent. Weight distribution is about 80-20.

Modification:

If you have back problems or are pregnant; you can slightly modify this form, so that you don't have to bend down or arch back. Body remains upright, just move forward as you scoop and backward as you lift.

Visualization:

You may visualize you are scooping all the positive energy from the sea; then the water from the sea travels down all over you cleansing your body at the same time.

12. Playing with Waves

Bring both hands at chest level.
Lift left toes up so that left heel is the only part
of the left foot that is touching the ground.

A. Push hands:

- breathing out
- palms facing forward
- push both hands out
- transfer weight to left foot
- right heel leaves the ground
- left foot completely on the ground

B. Pull hands back:

- breathing in
- palms face the ground
- pull back both hands to chest
- transfer weight from left foot to right
- right heel returns to the ground
- Lift left toes up so that the left heel is the only part of the left foot that is touching the ground

Repeat A-B 11 times, and then do A one final time

Common Mistakes:

1. Not sitting on the back leg

Weight distribution is about 90-10. When you move back, make sure you are sitting on the right leg, and your body remains upright, not leaning back.

2. Palms facing down when pushing out

When you push out, your palms should be facing out.

3. Overextending

Your body should remain upright as you push forward.

13. Spreading Your Wings

Turn palms to face each other.

A. Open arms:

- breathing in
- slightly bend elbows bringing arms slightly inward with palms facing body
- open both arms out to the sides
- transfer weight to right foot
- right heel returns to the ground
- lift left toes up so that the left heel is the only part of the left foot that is touching the ground

B. Close arms:

- breathing out
- close both arms in front to shoulder width apart
- transfer weight from right foot to left
- left foot completely on the ground
- right heel leaves the ground

Repeat A-B 12 times

1. Opposite arm movements

Your arms should open when you are sitting on your back leg, close when you are moving forward.

2. Arms remain straight when opening

Your hands should come slightly toward your body first, and then open.

3. Shoulders not relaxed

Make sure your shoulders are relaxed, otherwise after a few movements your shoulders will get tired already.

4. Not sitting on the back leg

Weight distribution is about 90-10. When you move back, make sure you are sitting on the right leg, and your body remains upright.

5. Opening the arms to the sides too late

You should start open the arms to the sides when your hands are about 4 fists away from your chest.

14. Punching

Breathe in as you bring the left leg back to its original position; drawing in both fists to the sides of the waist, fist-palms face up. Remain in horse riding stance throughout the entire movement.

A. Right punch out:

- breathing out
- punch right fist out straight ahead
- as you punch turn the fist-palm down

B. Pull right fist back:

- breathing in
- draw right fist back to waist
- as you pull back turn the fist-palm up

C. Left punch out:

- breathing out
- punch left fist out straight ahead
- as you punch turn the fist-palm down

D. Pull left fist back:

- breathing in
- draw left fist back to waist
- as you pull back turn the fist-palm up

Repeat A-D 3 times

Common Mistakes:

1. Feet at wrong position

When you step back, make sure your toes are still pointing forward and the stance is shoulder width.

2. Punching at the center

You punch just straight ahead.

3. Fist resting too high and not spiraling

The fists should be resting at the waist level fist palms facing up. When you punch, you slowly spiral your fist at the same time.

4. Squeeze the armpits

Make sure there is some space in your armpits.

5. Both fists are moving at the same time

Make sure the fist comes back first before you punch with the other hand.

6. Moving up and down

You should remain in the horse riding stance throughout the entire movement.

7. Thumb sticking out

Make sure the thumbs are
bent, not sticking out.

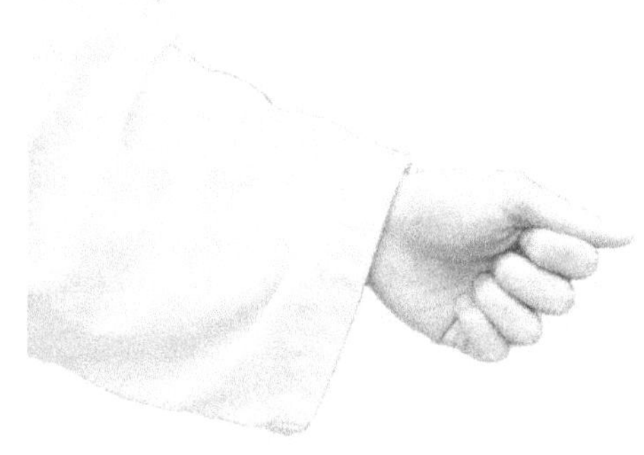

When you make the fists,
make sure the fists are
loose, not tight.

15. Flying like a Goose

Breathe out and lower arms to the front of thighs, palms face each other.

A. Raise heels:

- breathing in
- raise body
- raise heels off the ground
- both arms go out the sides up to head level
- palms face the ground
- elbows slightly bent

B. Lower heels:

- breathing out
- lower heels to the ground
- both arms return to front of thighs
- palms face each other
- knees slightly bent

Repeat A-B 6 times

1. Shoulders not relaxed

2. Arms go up too high

Just slightly above your head is good enough.

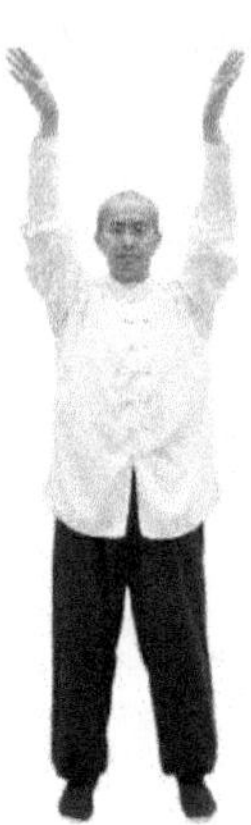

Visualization:

You may visualize you are a bird flying high in the sky.

16. Spinning Wheels

Bend down forward from waist. Palms face each other.

A. Circle clockwise up:

- breathing in
- raise body by twisting to the **left** and up
- raise arms from the left side until above the head
- tilt body arching slightly backwards

B. Circle clockwise down:

- breathing out
- lower both arms to the right side
- lower body by twisting to the right
- bend down from waist

Repeat A-B 3 times

C. Circle counter-clockwise up:

- breathing in
- raise body by twisting to the **right** and up
- raise arms from the right side until above the head
- tilt body arching slightly backward

D. Circle counter-clockwise down:

- breathing out
- lower both arms to the left side
- lower body by twisting to the left
- bend down from waist

Repeat C-D 3 times

Common Mistakes:

1. Bending the knees

You are just turning from your waist; no need
to bend your knees.

2. Movements are initiated by arms

Movements should be generated from waist.

Modification:

People who have back problems or are pregnant can modify the form by just
turning from one side to the other.   No need to bend down or arch back.

17. Bouncing a Ball

Slowly return body upright, and pause for a second or two.

A. Right bounce up:

- breathing in
- shift weight to right foot
- raise right hand to slightly above shoulder
- raise left knee until left thigh is almost parallel with ground
- bounce once on the right foot (raise and lower heel)

B. Back down:

- bring right arm down
- put left toes down then left heel down

C. Left bounce up:

- breathing out
- shift the weight to left foot
- raise left hand to slightly above shoulder
- raise right knee until right thigh almost parallel with ground
- bounce once on the left foot (raise and lower heel)

D. Back down:

- bring left arm down
- put right toes down then right heel down

Repeat A-D 6 times

Common Mistakes:

1. Moving the knees up to the center

Your knee should only go up vertically.

2. Lifting the wrong leg

You should be lifting either the left arm with right leg, or right arm with left leg together.

3. Crouching the back

Make sure you are upright and your spine is straight.

Modification:

For those who have a problem maintaining balance, just lift your feet up a little bit to your own comfort level. When your balance improves, you can lift higher.

The keys to maintain balance in this movement:

1. Make sure your spine is straight.

2. Do not look down at the floor; you just look straight ahead.

18. Pressing the Palms

A. Raise qi:

- breathing in
- raise body
- turn palms to face up
- gently raise hands upwards and slightly out until palms face the nose

B. Ground qi:

- breathing out
- bring palms in toward body
- lower hands downwards to waist level
- palms face down
- sink body with knees slightly bent

Repeat A-B 6 times

Common Mistakes:

1. Hands too far away from body when pressing down

Your hands come toward your body first before they go down.

2. Fingers pointing forward when pressing down

Fingers should be pointing toward each other when pressing down.

3. Body not moving up and down

Make sure you are raising your body when inhaling and lowering when exhaling.

This final movement gathers the qi back to your lower dan tian. If for some reason you have to stop in the middle of the form, you should do this last movement a few times; and then you can walk away to do whatever you need. Otherwise, you will waste some of the qi you have generated.

Closing Position (Holding the Qi Ball)

- stand with feet shoulder width apart, knees slightly bent
- relax the whole body
- arms hang down bowed as if holding a ball
- palms face lower dan tian
- remain in this posture for a few minutes

Common Mistakes:

1. Fingers too tense

Make sure your fingers are relaxed.

2. Palms not facing lower dan tian

Make sure there is some space in your armpits.

You are consolidating the qi you gathered in this step.

Playing with the Qi Ball (optional)

Move hands slowly apart and then together. Practice separating your hands in different directions. You should feel some sensation between your palms.

This exercise trains your sensitivity to qi.

Final Position (Sealing the Qi)

Place hands on lower dan tian.

Men right hand over left.

Women left hand over right.

Tai Chi Qigong Shibashi Set 2 Introduction

Tai Chi Qigong Shibashi Set 2 was created in the same year and by the same team as Set 1. One of the key contributors to this set is Master He Weiqi, from whom I learned this form during my time in Shanghai. Master He, along with Jet Li (who later became a famous movie star), was invited by President Richard Nixon to perform Wushu at the White House in 1974. Her Wushu background introduced some martial arts elements into Set 2, giving it a slightly different flavor compared to the first set.

While most movements in Tai Chi Qigong Shibashi Set 1 are stationary, Set 2 introduces more dynamic stepping—such as moving to the sides, stepping back, and standing on one leg. These movements are excellent for developing lower body strength and improving balance, both of which are vital as we age.

As we grow older, the legs are often the first to show signs of weakness, as they are farthest from the heart. Additionally, our sense of balance tends to decline with age, making it even more important to engage in exercises that target these areas. To test and improve your balancing ability, you may find this short video helpful: 1-Minute Fall Prevention Exercise (https://youtu.be/XsODC4ovmgc). The more intricate movements of Set 2 also enhance full-body coordination, offering a comprehensive workout for both the body and mind.

Here is the link to the Tai Chi Qigong Shibashi Set 2 Video:
https://youtu.be/NOENwWg3e2M

How to Practice

Since Set 2 is more physically demanding than Set 1, it's important not to push yourself beyond your comfort zone. Practice the movements at your own pace, doing your best while avoiding strain. It's recommended to perform Set 1 as a warm-up before moving on to Set 2. If you prefer to practice Set 2 on its own, begin with some warm-up exercise such as the *Silk Reeling Exercise* https://www.taichi18.com/online-video-course/silk to stretch your tendons and loosen your joints.

Apply the same breathing method (abdominal breathing) as in Set 1. Many of the common mistakes for this set are similar to those in Set 1, so I have grouped them into the *"Things to Notice"* section under each movement.

Nei Jin

Once you are comfortable with all the movements in this set, you can incorporate an optional practice to develop your nei jin (inner strength). Nei jin differs from muscular force; it requires your muscles and tendons to stay relaxed even while generating power. This concept is unique to internal martial arts like Tai Chi.

To develop nei jin, visualize yourself moving through water during the form. Imagine encountering gentle resistance with each movement, as though the water is pushing back slightly. The key is to stay relaxed and avoid tensing your muscles. This simple mental imagery helps cultivate inner force while maintaining fluidity and balance.

Opening Position (Wuji Stance)

- Stand with your feet parallel, shoulder width apart.
- Create a little space in your armpits.
- Let your arms hang down at your sides; palms facing your thighs.
- Gently pull up from the Bai hui (top of the head), and slightly tuck in your chin.
- Bend your knees slightly.
- Tuck in your tailbone.
- Clear your mind.
- Relax your whole body.
- Breathe naturally.
- Remain in this posture for a few minutes.

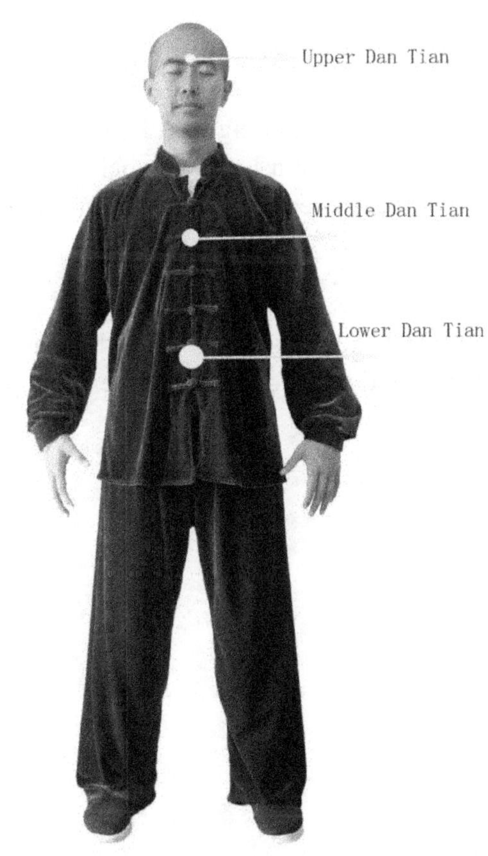

1. Regulating the Qi

A. Breathing in:

- Raise your body by straightening your knees, and
- Raise your arms toward your head with palms facing down.
- When then hands reach head level, palms naturally facing out.

B. Breathing out:
- Lower your body, bending knees to about 150° and
- Circle hands out, and then down to the sides with palms facing down

Repeat A-B 6 times

Optional Practice:

During the Wuji stance, visualize your hands and arms extending deeply into the ground, connecting with the Earth's energy. Once you feel this connection, begin the movement.

As you lift your arms, imagine drawing Earth's energy up through your body, starting from your feet. Feel it rising to the Bai Hui (top of the head), then expanding outward.

If you have high blood pressure, do not guide the energy beyond the middle Dan Tian. Instead, direct it to the middle Dan Tian and let it expand outward from there, or skip this part entirely.

Things to notice:

- When your arms go up, make sure your shoulders are relaxed; especially when your arms go higher than your shoulders.
- When lowering your body, make sure your knees do not go beyond your toes.

2. Moving the Qi along the Microcosmic Orbit

Gently bring your palms together in prayer position, fingers pointing down, with your wrists in front of the lower dan tian. Palms are loosely touching.

A. Breathing in:
- Raise your body as you
- Raise your hands upward to the middle dan tian, then
- Rotate your hands to point up, and continue to raise them to the upper dan tian

B. Breathing out:

- Lower your body
- Pushing your prayer hands forward and rotating them to point down as they arc toward the lower dan tian

Repeat A-B 6 times

Things to Notice:

- When your hands go up, make sure you don't raise your shoulders.
- Leave some space in the armpits so that the energy can easily travel between the arms and the body.
- Hands should not go higher than your head.

In China, moving qigong is traditionally called Dao Yin. Dao Yin means guiding the qi. If you do this movement correctly, you should feel the energy traveling up along your spine to the head, then back down through the front of your body completing the microcosmic orbit.

I do not recommend that you <u>visualize</u> the energy traveling in this fashion. If your energy channels are clear, you do the movements correctly, your mind is calm enough, and your body is relaxed enough; then the energy will automatically travel this way.

It is not necessary to use the mind to guide qi at this level. Deliberately using the mind to guide energy, especially above your neck or to the head can be troublesome. Many people have a difficult time guiding the energy through the narrow jade pillow gate (point on the back of the head).

If the conditions are not ready, and you force the energy to pass through that gate; then qi may find some detours or even get stuck somewhere. If that happens, it may cause headaches, or you may feel something heavy in your head. This could last for days, months, or even years!

3. Wind Blowing the Willows

Separate your hands to the sides of your body.

A. Breathing in:
- Transfer your weight to the right leg
- Step forward 45 degrees to the left with your left foot, resting it on the heel (only on the first time)
- Raising the left foot onto its heel (skip this step on the first time)
- At the same time reach forward and up with your right hand, palm facing up; reach backward and down with the left hand, palm facing back, and
- Your head naturally follows your body turning slightly to the left

B. Breathing out:

- Transfer weight to your left leg with left foot completely on the ground
- At the same time reach forward and up with the left hand, palm facing up; reach backward and down with the right hand, palm facing back, and
- Your head naturally follows your body turning slightly to the right

Repeat A-B 3 times

Step back with the left leg to the original position as you inhale.

C. Breathing in:

- Transfer your weight to your left leg
- Step forward 45 degrees to the right with your right foot, resting it on the heel (only on the first time)
- Raising the right foot onto its heel (skip this step on the first time)
- Reach forward and up with the left hand, palm facing up; reach backward and down with the right hand, palm facing back, and
- Your head naturally follows your body turning slightly to the right

D. Breathing out:

- Transfer weight to your right leg with right foot completely on the ground
- At the same time reach forward and up with the right hand, palm facing up; reach backward and down with the left hand, palm facing back, and
- Your head naturally follows your body turning slightly to the left

Repeat C-D 3 times

Things to Notice:

- Make sure you are stepping 45 degrees to your side, not completely sideways.
- Keep the step small, aligning the heel of one foot with the toes of the other.
- The transition from B to C is smooth and seamless.
- Keep your arms relaxed, like supple willow branches swaying gently in the wind.

4. Searching for Needles in the Sea

A. Breathing in:

- Step the right leg back to the original position (skip this step when repeating)
- Straighten-up your body, and bring your left leg back to the original position (skip this the first time)
- Bring your hands in to the front of the middle dan tian (hands face each other, pointing slightly up) as you shift your weight to the right leg

B. Breathing out:

- Take a small step forward with your left leg 45 degrees to the left, keeping the heel slightly off the ground
- Bend forward as you lower your parallel hands down in front of the body; then continue down along the sides of your left thigh and calf, with fingers pointing down

C. Breathing in:

- Straighten-up your body, and bring left leg back to the original position
- At the same time, bring your hands in to the front of the middle dan tian (hands face each other, pointing slightly up) and shift your weight to the left leg

D. Breathing out:

- Take a small step forward with your right leg 45 degrees to the right, keeping the heel slightly off the ground
- Bend forward as you lower your parallel hands down in front of the body; then continue down along the sides of your right thigh and calf, with fingers pointing down

Repeat A-D 3 times

<u>Things to Notice:</u>

- Whenever you take a step, your weight is on the back leg.
- When you step forward, make sure the heel of the outstretched foot is a little off the ground.
- As your hands move down your front leg, bend forward smoothly and evenly from the spine and hips. Keep the weight on the back leg.

Visualize/feel all the bad qi and toxins in your body moving downward and exiting deep into the ground through the bottom of your front foot. As you breathe out and move your hands downward, your hands are pushing the negative elements out of your body.

73

5. Fisherman Casting the Net

Remain in horse riding stance throughout this movement with your knees bending at about 150°.

A. Breathing in:
- With elbows just slightly bent, bring both arms up to the front of the body and step back to horse riding stance (skip this step when repeating)
- Turn your palms to face the left (left arm should be higher than the right)
- At the same time, turn your body left as you gently glide both hands to the left, keeping the left hand higher
- Your head follows your hands

B. Breathing out:

- Switch the position of your hands (right is higher), turn your palms to face right
- At the same time, turn your body right as you gently glide both hands to the right, keeping the right hand higher
- Your head follows your hands

Repeat A-B 6 times

Things to Notice:

- Relax the shoulders and elbows, especially the higher arm.
- Make sure you have some space in the armpits.
- The top hand should finish at about shoulder level; the other hand is lower.
- Remain in the horse riding stance, and turn your body from the waist; don't move your body up and down.

6. Immortal Pointing the Way

Sword Fingers: The index and middle fingers point straight forward. The ring and little fingers curl into the palm, and the thumb rests on top of them.

A. Breathing in:

- Step back to the original position as you release the sword fingers (skip this step the first time)
- Circle both arms clockwise, down to the left, then up around to the right
- Turn body from left to right in conjunction with hands

B. Breathing out:

- Form sword fingers with both hands
- Step the right foot diagonally back past the left leg; touching the ground with the just ball and toes of the foot
- As you step, slide sword fingers across your body horizontally and back to the left while lowering your body
- Keep weight at the left leg
- Turn your head to the left following the sword fingers

C. Breathing in:

- Step back to the original position as you release the sword fingers
- Circle both arms counter-clockwise down to the right, then up around to the left
- Turn body from right to left in conjunction with hands

D. Breathing out:

- Form sword fingers with both hands
- Step the left foot diagonally back past the right leg; touching the ground with the just ball and toes of the foot
- As you step, slide sword fingers across your body horizontally and back to the right while lowering your body
- Keep weight at the right leg.
- Turn your head to the right following the sword fingers

Repeat A-D 3 times

Things to Notice:

- When circling your arms clockwise, start and end at 3 o'clock.
- When circling your arms counter-clockwise, start and end at 9 o'clock.
- When you step back, your hands (sword fingers) are moving at the same time.
- Be sure when you are pointing, it is further back than 90 degrees.
- If you find this movement too demanding, during steps B & D use a smaller step and do not go too low.

7. Mischievous Boy Kicking his Legs

Step back to the original position, and place both hands on your waist.

A. Breathing in:
- Shift your weight to your right leg and
- Lift your left knee up so that it bends at 90°

B. Breathing out

- Slowly push your left heel forward and down towards the ground as you
- Lower your body

C. Breathing in:

- Straighten right leg as you
- Lift your left knee up so that it bends at 90°

D. Breathing out:

- Return the left leg to the original position

E. Breathing in:

- Shift your weight to your left leg and
- Lift your right knee up so that it bends at 90°

F. Breathing out:

- Slowly push your right heel forward and down towards the ground as you
- Lower your body

G. Breathing in:

- Straighten the left leg as you
- Lift your right knee up so that it bends at 90°

H. Breathing out:

- Return the right leg to the original position

Repeat A-H 3 times

Things to Notice:

- When pushing your leg forward and down, make sure to kick from the heel with your toes up.
- When you kick, lower your body with the supporting leg.
- Keep your shoulders relaxed.

For those who have problems maintaining balance, do not lift your leg too high in steps A, C, E and G. You may touch your heel to the floor for steps B and F. As you practice this movement, you will build up more strength and stamina in your lower body; then you should be able to do this movement the original way.

8. Holy Crane Worshiping the Moon

A. Breathing in:

- Raise your body stepping back to original position (skip this step the first time)
- Open your arms down to the sides;
- *Keep your weight to the right leg while (optional)*
- Turning your body *and left leg* (*optional*) slightly to the right
- Circle both arms up from sides, palms facing up, until just above your head;
- Shift your weight to your left leg, and step diagonally back with your right leg, placing only the ball and toes of your right foot on the ground

B. Breathing out:
- Bring both hands together in prayer position at the upper dan tian
- Lower your hands to the middle dan tian as you
- Lower your body until the right knee almost touches the ground

C. Breathing in:

- Raise your body stepping back to original position
- Open your arms down to the sides;
- *Keep your weight to the left leg while (optional)*
- Turning your body *and right leg (optional)* slightly to the left;
- Circle both arms up from sides, palms facing up, until just above your head;
- Shift your weight to your right leg, and step diagonally back with your left leg, placing only the ball and toes of your left foot on the ground

D. Breathing out:
- Bring both hands together in prayer position at the upper dan tian
- Lower your hands to the middle dan tian as you
- Lower your body until the left knee almost touches the ground

Repeat A-D 3 times

Things to Notice:

- Step back first then lower your body. (This is different than Immortal Pointing the Way which you slide back and lower your body at the same time.)
- In prayer posture make sure you leave some space in your armpits, and a little space between your prayer hands and your body.
- Ideally your fingers should point straight up in prayer posture.
- This movement places more demand on the knees. If you experience any discomfort, you can:
1. Avoid going too low during steps B and D.
2. When raising your body, engage your **kua** (pelvis) to push forward rather than relying on your knees. A video link in the next movement demonstrates how to perform this technique.
3. Opt to follow the optional steps indicated in *italics*.

9. Yellow Dragon Pushing Out with Claws

Assume horse riding stance with feet parallel, shoulder width apart, and knees bending to about 130° or lower.

A. Breathing in:

- Raise your body as you
- Make two fists, and pull them upward in front of the body to just above the middle dan tian

B. Breathing out:

- Lower your body to horse riding stance and
- Open the fists and slightly curve your fingers so that they look like claws
- Push both hands out from your chest in a slightly upward arc,
- Continue to arc your hands downward to your thighs*

Repeat A-B 6 times

*On the last repetition, circle the hands out to the sides as they go down to the thighs.

<u>Things to Notice:</u>

- The fists are half-closed, not tightly closed.
- Push with the outside edge of your hands; thus your palms (claws) are not directly facing the front.
- When pushing out, be sure the hands arc slightly up rather than straight out.
- When pulling the fists upward, make sure shoulders are relaxed; and leave some space in your armpits.

If possible, try to adopt a lower stance in this movement to build the strength and stamina of your lower body. The lower body is like the roots of a tree: when the roots are weak, the tree cannot stand strong or endure for long. Similarly, a weak lower body can compromise your balance, stability, and overall vitality. As we age, weakness often begins in the lower body because it is the furthest part from the heart and circulatory system.

You might have noticed that many babies instinctively kick their legs, a clear sign of vitality. Teenagers, brimming with energy, often shake their legs as if they cannot contain their vigor. In contrast, as we grow older, our habits change: we tend to cross our legs, unconsciously conserving qi, and eventually may rely on a "third leg"—a walking stick—for support. This progression highlights the importance of strengthening the lower body to maintain balance, vitality, and overall health.

Much like blood, **qi** has greater difficulty reaching the extremities, particularly the lower body, as we age. This is why the meridians in the legs are generally harder to keep open compared to those in the arms. As a result, many older people tend to have weaker legs despite maintaining relatively strong arms. A simple yet effective way to promote the free circulation of blood and **qi** in the lower body is to adopt a lower stance during Shibashi movements. This lower stance not only activates the muscles in the lower body but also enhances the flow of energy through the meridians.

When practicing with a lower stance, it is crucial to pay close attention to your posture to protect your knees from injury. Ensure that your knees are aligned with your toes and do not extend beyond them. Avoid sticking out your bottom, and keep your upper body upright. These adjustments help you maintain proper alignment, reduce unnecessary strain on your joints, and enhance the effectiveness of the movement.

If you find this challenging, it may be due to a lack of openness in your kua (hip joints/pelvic region). Opening the kua is crucial for optimizing movement, improving balance, and reducing stress on the knees. To help with this, the *Qigong Mode and Tai Chi Requirements* series offers a variety of exercises, ranging from beginner to advanced levels, designed to fully open the kua and strengthen the lower body.

For a practical demonstration, here is a video that teaches you how to use the kua effectively: https://youtu.be/cCx82sXERCI. By learning to utilize your kua properly, you can alleviate knee problems, enhance mobility, and foster better overall health. With consistent practice, you will develop greater strength, stamina, and balance in your lower body, laying a strong foundation—like the roots of a tree—for lifelong vitality.

10. Pulling the Bow to Shoot the Eagle

Remember: On the previous move, circle hands out to
the sides as they go down to the thighs.

A. Breathing in:

- Raise your body (only on the first time)
- Raise both arms upward in front of the midline of
  your body to the upper dan tian (palms up, fingers
  forward)

B. Breathing out:

- Rotate both hands so that palms face outward while
- Shifting your weight to the right leg, and turning your
  head to the left
- Separate your hands: Fully extend the left arm out to the left then down
  to the thigh; and circle your right arm, with elbow bent, out to the right
  then down to the thigh as you
- Shift weight back to center with knees slightly bent

C. Breathing in:

- Raise both arms upward in front of the midline of your body to the upper dan tian (palms up, fingers forward)

D. Breathing out:

- Rotate both hands so that palms face outward while
- Shifting your weight to the left leg, and turning your head to the right
- Separate your hands: Fully extend the right arm to the right, then down to the thigh; and circle your left arm, with the elbow bent, out to the left then down to the thigh as you
- Shift weight back to center with knees slightly bent

Repeat A-D 3 times

Things to Notice:

- When shifting your weight to one side, make sure your body remains upright, not leaning.
- When separating your hands, the extended hand faces to the side while extending out, and the other hand faces forward. Both hands face down when they are moving down to the thighs.
- When you are lifting your arms up, make sure to keep some space in the armpits.

11. Twin Dragons Emerging from the Sea

Bend each middle finger to touch the corresponding thumb.

A. Breathing in:
- Shift your weight to the right leg as you
- Lift both arms forward and up until they are slightly above your head with palms facing up

B. Breathing out:
- Turn your body 45 degrees to the left and step forward with the left leg (only on the first time)
- Shift your weight to the left leg and
- Circle your hands toward you, under your armpits, and fully extend your arms toward the back and down as you lean forward

Repeat A-B 3 times

C. Breathing in:

- Shifting your weight to the right leg; then step back with left leg as you turn your body to the right (only on the first time)
- Shift your weight to the left leg as you
- Lift both arms forward and up until they are slightly above your head with palms facing up

D. Breathing out:

- Step forward 45 degrees to the right with the right leg, turning your body to the right (only on the first time)
- Shift your weight to the right leg and
- Circle your hands toward you, under your armpits, and fully extend your arms toward the back and down as you lean forward

Repeat C-D 3 times

Things to Notice:

- Make sure you are stepping at 45 degrees to your side, not completely sideways.
- The step shouldn't be too big; just a half step is enough.
- When changing direction, your hands keep doing the same motion while you step and turn.
- During steps B, D there are two forces moving at opposite directions. As your arms are moving backward and down, your body is going forward and up. Your body and arms form a diagonal line. When you do this, try to feel each vertebrate of your spine opening; and your whole body extending forward and up.

12. Crossing the Wild Blue Ocean

Begin here the first time:

A. Breathing in:
- Right foot steps back
- Raise your arms to chest level, bringing them to your chest
- Pivot on your left heel as you turn your body toward the left, and turn palms facing out (keeping toes pointing up)
- Continue to step 'B'

*Begin repetitions here:

A. Breathing in:

- Shift weight back to the left leg (foot flat on the floor); right foot raises onto its heel as you
- Turn your body to the left by first pivoting on your right heel, then pivoting on the left heel while
- Circling arms (palms facing down) back to your chest, and then palms facing out (fingers up)

B. Breathing out:

- Push forward and slightly up with both palms
- Shifting your weight forward onto the left leg so that foot is completely on the floor, and the right heel is lifted

C. Breathing in:

- Shift weight back to the right leg (foot flat on the floor); left foot raises onto its heel, as you
- Turn your body to the right by first pivoting on your left heel, then pivoting on the right heel while
- Circling arms (palms facing down) back to your chest, and then palms facing out (fingers up)

D. Breathing out:

- Push forward and slightly up with both palms
- Shifting your weight forward onto the right leg so that foot is completely on the floor, and the left heel is lifted

Repeat *A-D 3 times

Things to Notice:

- When pivoting on the left heel, weight is on the right leg.
- When pivoting on the right heel, weight is on the left leg.
- Pivot your feet to the direction your body turns.
- After you push out, almost all the weight is on the forward foot.

13. Lion Playing with a Ball

A. Breathing in:

- Shift weight to the left leg
- Turn your body left by pivoting on the right heel, then pivoting on the left heel
- As you turn, move your left hand to the lower dan tian, palm facing up, and your right hand to the middle dan tian, palm facing down (as if holding a ball)
- Drag the left foot in, keeping toes on the floor, then lift the knee

B. Breathing out:

- Step forward to the left with the left leg, landing heel then toe and
- Shift your weight and body forward by bending the left knee
- At the same time, your left hand rotates to face out as it rises above the head and your right hand pushes out

C. Breathing in:

- Shift weight to the right leg
- Turn your body right by pivoting on the left heel, then pivoting on the right heel
- As you turn, move your right hand to the lower dan tian, palm facing up, and your left hand to the middle dan tian, palm facing down (as if holding a ball)
- Drag the right foot in, keeping toes on the floor, then lift the knee

D. Breathing out:

- Step forward to the right with the right leg, landing heel then toe and
- Shift your weight and body forward by bending the right knee
- At the same time, your right hand rotates to face out as it rises above the head and your left hand pushes out

Repeat A-D 3 times

<u>Things to Notice:</u>

- When you're turning, your hands are coming in to hold the ball.
- Hold the ball with the upper hand slightly above the middle dan tian and the lower hand slightly below the lower dan tian.
- As you step forward, your lower hand rises to block, and your upper hand pushes forward.
- Make sure you leave some space in your armpits when holding the ball in front of you.

14. Embracing the Moon at the Dan Tian

Shift your weight to the left leg, and step the right foot back to the original position. Check to make sure your stance is shoulder width apart. Lower both arms to the sides and sink your body.

A. Breathing in:

- Turn your body to the left as you raise your body, and
- Circle your arms out as if reaching up to the left to embrace the big moon

B. Breathing out:

- Turn to the front as you lower your body, and
- Bring your hands close together to your lower dan tian as if you are carrying the moon from up above to your lower dan tian

C. Breathing in:

- Turn your body to the right as you raise your body, and
- Circle your arms out as if reaching up to the right to embrace the big moon

D. Breathing out:

- Turn to the front as you lower your body, and
- Bring your hands close together to your lower dan tian as if you are carrying the moon from up above to your lower dan tian

Repeat A-D 3 times

Things to Notice:

- During steps A and C, you open your arms first, then hug the moon (or energy ball) as you carry it back to center. You can visualize opening your arms up to embrace the moon.
- During steps B and D imagine you are making the moon smaller, and then placing it into your lower dan tian.
- Try to adopt a lower stance, but make sure your knees don't go beyond the toes.

15. Phoenix Spreading its Wings

A. Breathing in:

- Turn your body to the left
- Shifting your weight to the left leg, and lifting your right heel as you raise your body while
- Swinging both arms up and out to the sides - head height, palms facing down (like a bird flapping its wings)

B. Breathing out:

- Turn your body back toward the front, lowering the right heel
- Shifting your weight to the center, sinking the body while
- Swinging your arms back down until hands are alongside the body

C. Breathing in:

- Turn your body to the right
- Shifting your weight to the right leg, and lifting your left heel as you raise your body while
- Swinging both arms up and out to the sides - head height, palms facing down

D. Breathing out:

- Turn your body back toward the front, lowering the left heel
- Shifting your weight to the center, sinking the body while
- Swinging your arms back down until hands are alongside the body

Repeat A-D 3 times

16. Striking the Opponent's Ears

A. Breathing in:

- Form two lightly clenched fists alongside of your waist, palms up and elbows pointing back

B. Breathing out:

- Shift your weight to the right leg; turn your body slightly to the left, rotating the fists so that the front of your fists are facing your body, and elbows point to the sides
- Step forward 45 degrees to the left with your left leg, and then shift your weight to that leg
- At the same time, rotate your fists upward and outward in an extended arc to head level so fists face each other; as if 'striking the opponent's ears'

C. Breathing in: (* begin repetitions here)

- Shift weight to the right leg, and step back with the left leg, centering your weight as you
- Circle both fists back toward the body reversing the path and placing fists alongside the waist; palms up and elbows pointing back

D. Breathing out:

- Shift your weight to the left leg, and turn your body slightly to the right; as you rotate the fists so that the front of your fists are facing your body, and elbows point to the sides
- Step forward to the right 45 degrees with your right leg, and then shift your weight to that leg
- As you step, rotate your fists upward and outward in an extended arc to head level so fists face each other; as if 'striking the opponent's ears'

E. Breathing in:

- Shift your weight to the left leg, and step back with the right leg, centering your weight as you
- Circle both fists back toward the body reversing the path and placing fists alongside the waist; palms up and elbows pointing back

F. Breathing out:

- Shift your weight to the right leg, and turn your body slightly to the left; as you rotate the fists so that the front of your fists are facing your body, and elbows point to the sides
- Step forward to the left 45 degrees with your left leg, and then shift your weight to that leg
- As you step, rotate your fists upward and outward in an extended arc to head level so fists face each other; as if 'striking the opponent's ears'

Repeat *C-F 2 times

Things to Notice:

- When your fists are at the waist, your wrists touch the sides of your waist; so the fists are actually in front of your sides.
- Do not squeeze your arms into your body when placing the fists alongside the waist.
- Your arms circle forward and back as you step forward and back.

17. Circling the Qi around the Dan Tian

Step back to original position and lower to horse riding stance.

With palms facing down, bring both hands down in front of your lower dan tian.

A. Move both hands counter-clockwise as if outlining a circle

B. Move your lower dan tian in a smaller circle in conjunction with your hands

Repeat A-B 6 times

C. Move both hands clockwise as if outlining a circle

D. Move your lower dan tian in a smaller circle in conjunction with your hands

Repeat C-D 6 times

Things to Notice:

- Remain in the horse riding stance throughout this movement.
- Relax the kua.
- When circling hands, breathe out when pushing your hands away from the lower dan tian; and breathe in when bringing hands toward the lower dan tian.
- Remember to leave some space in the armpits.

The key to performing this movement lies not in simply moving the arms but in allowing the lower dan tian to internally generate the motion, with the arms naturally following its lead. In Tai Chi, all movements originate from the dan tian, as the limbs are intrinsically connected to this central energy hub. When the dan tian initiates the movement from within, the limbs flow effortlessly, embodying the harmony between internal energy and external expression.

To begin developing this vital connection, you may initially need to consciously emphasize the circling motion of your lower dan tian. This helps establish awareness of the internal dynamics. As your practice deepens and you begin to feel the energetic link between your dan tian and your limbs, the outward movement of the dan tian can gradually become subtler. Over time, the motion refines itself to the point where it is almost imperceptible, with all the work happening internally—a hallmark of advanced Tai Chi practice.

This movement originates from a *qigong* system known as Tai Chi Ruler or Tai Chi Stick, which traditionally involves repeating the same motion for over half an hour. If you have more time, you can go beyond the typical six repetitions and perform this movement as many times as you like to fully reap its benefits. Firstly, it helps establish and strengthen the connection between your *dan tian* and your limbs, fostering a harmonious integration of internal and external movement. Secondly, it builds and nourishes the energy within your lower *dan tian*, an essential reservoir for vitality and overall well-being. Finally, it cultivates mindfulness by grounding your awareness in the present moment—a skill that transcends physical practice and enriches every aspect of your daily life.

Interestingly, this movement reflects the story of the Sixth Patriarch of Zen, Hui Neng (638–713 CE), one of the most revered figures in Chinese Zen history. Before his enlightenment, Hui Neng was an illiterate laborer tasked with grinding rice in the temple kitchen. For years, he stood in front of the grinding tool, turning it tirelessly—a repetitive and seemingly mundane motion that mirrors the simplicity of this qigong movement.

Yet, it was during one of these humble tasks that Hui Neng experienced a profound awakening. The repetitive rhythm of grinding rice, combined with his inner focus and dedication, became a catalyst for his enlightenment. Following this transformative moment, Hui Neng composed numerous profound Zen teachings and poems, transcending his earlier limitations and becoming a luminous figure in spiritual history.

This story beautifully demonstrates how even the simplest movements, when performed with mindfulness, dedication, and inner focus, can lead to extraordinary transformations. Like Hui Neng's rice-grinding, this movement invites practitioners to discover the profound within the ordinary and to transform simplicity into a pathway to deeper wisdom and vitality.

18. Collecting the Qi

Lower your palms in front of the body.

A. Breathing in:

- Raise the body and
- Turn your palms up, circling your hands up and out to the sides of your body
- At head level, your hands come inward and begin to face down

B. Breathing out:

- Lower the body and
- Press your hands down, returning them to the lower dan tian (palms face down with fingers pointing to each other)

Repeat A-B 6 times

On the last repetition, bring your hands in to face your lower dan tian

Things to Notice:

- This movement gathers the qi back to the lower dan tian.

Closing Position (Holding the Qi Ball Stance)

- Stand with your feet parallel, shoulder width apart
- Palms face the lower dan tian as if holding a large ball of qi
- Gently pull up from the Bai hui and slightly tuck in your chin
- Sink your body (the lower the better)
- Slightly tuck in your tailbone
- Clear your mind
- Relax your body
- Remain in this posture for at least 5 minutes (the longer the better)

Closing Techniques

Playing with the Qi Ball (optional)

Move hands slowly apart and then together. Practice separating your hands in different directions. You should feel some sensation between your palms.

This exercise trains your sensitivity to qi.

Sealing the Qi

Place hands on lower dan tian (men right hand over left; women left hand over right)

Put your attention inside the lower dan tian for at least one minute.

Massaging and Patting

Rub your hands together vigorously until the palms are warm.

A. Massaging your face and head:

- Glide your ring fingers from the sides of your nostrils; up the center of your face to your forehead
- Then comb your fingers through your hair to the back of your neck
- Your hands return to your face; ring fingers at the sides of your nose

Repeat 18 times

B. Patting your body:

- Cross your arms at your chest and pat both shoulders
- Pat down the inside of the right arm and back up along the outside to the shoulder
- Pat down the inside of the left arm and back up along the outside to the shoulder
- With both hands pat down the chest to the hips
- Continue patting down the insides of the legs to your feet and
- Pat around the ankles to the back; then up the backs of your legs to your kidneys
- Gently strike up and down the kidney area with your hands

This part prevents qi stagnate in any part of your body, especially your head.

Ending Notes

I am confident that you will benefit from practicing these two Qigong sets. Thousands of practitioners have shared their transformative experiences with just Set 1 alone! The key to success lies in your dedication—make this a daily habit. Just 15 minutes a day is enough to bring noticeable improvements.

If you wish to explore the deeper aspects of Qigong and uncover the subtle details behind these movements, I encourage you to delve further. This includes learning how to:

- Enter a deep Qigong healing state of mind,

- Integrate Daoist Dan Tian breathing seamlessly into your movements,

- Relax your muscles and joints without compromising body posture,

- Achieve a lightness in your arms, making them feel as though they are floating effortlessly.

- And much more …

For a deeper understanding, I highly recommend the _Qigong Mode and Tai Chi Posture Requirement_ course.

Not sure if you're performing the movements correctly? We offer one-on-one online Zoom classes and have certified instructors worldwide who regularly teach _Tai Chi Qigong Shibashi_ Sets 1 and 2, check our website for details taichi18.com

The Home Study Courses We Offer

Level	Beginner (Level 1)	Intermediate (Level 2) - *for those who have mastered the basic skills from the Qigong Mode & Tai Chi Posture Requirements Level 1 Course*	Advance (Level 3) - *for those who are familiar with the techniques from the Qigong Mode & Tai Chi Posture Requirements Level 2 Course*
Core Courses	Tai Chi Qigong Shibashi Set 1 & Qigong Mode & Tai Chi Posture Requirements Level 1	Tai Chi Qigong Shibashi Set 2 & Qigong Mode & Tai Chi Posture Requirements Level 2	Tai Chi Neigong & Qigong Mode & Tai Chi Posture Requirements Level 3
Elective Courses	Hua Shan Healing Qigong: *focus on breathing practice* & Silk Reeling Exercise: *focus on body alignment & joints opening*	Yi Jin Jing: *focus on tendons and power training* & Awaken Lower Dan Tian by Tai Chi Push Hand: *A 2-person interactive qigong practice*	Solar Qigong: *meditative qigong focus on training the mind & spirit* & Certified Tai Chi Qigong Instructor Correspondence Courses Level 1 & 2: *teacher training programs*

Tai Chi and Qigong for Health Series: *These courses contain practical TCM information, along with various preventative and therapeutic techniques for some specific organs or illnesses. Suitable for all levels.*

Curriculum of our School

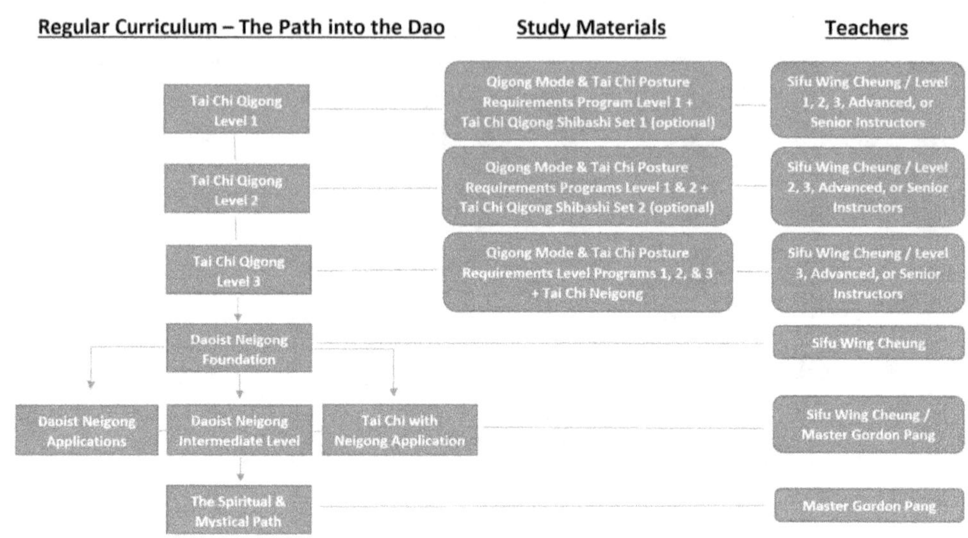

Tai Chi Qigong Instructor Certification Curriculum

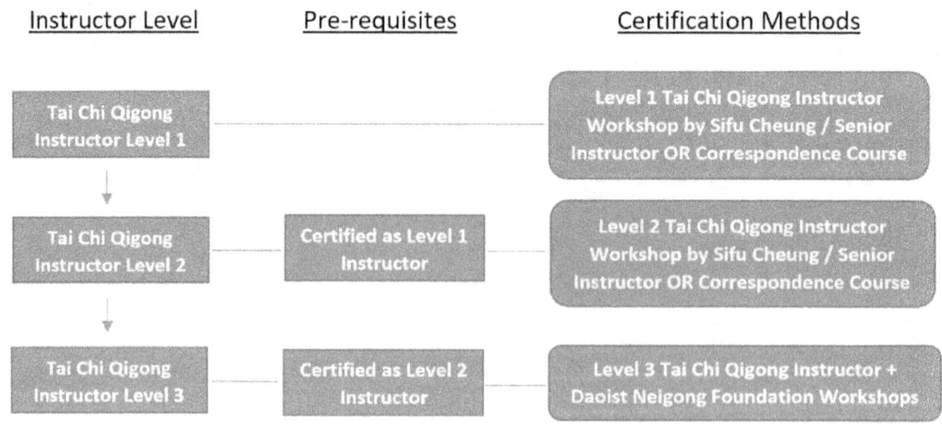

www.ingramcontent.com/pod-product-compliance
Lightning Source LLC
Chambersburg PA
CBHW051503050726
47593CB00005B/2205